Become A Client Magnet

27

STRATEGIES TO BOOST YOUR
CLIENT-ATTRACTION FACTOR

SANDY SCHUSSEL

Robert D. Reed Publishers ● Bandon, OR

Robert D. Reed Publishers
P.O. Box 1992
Bandon, OR 97411
Phone: 541-347-9882; Fax: -9883
E-mail: 4bobreed@msn.com
Website: www.rdrpublishers.com

Cover Designer: Cleone L. Reed
Book Designer: Debby Gwaltney
Copy Editor: Madeline Blue Schussel
Back Cover Photo: Sybil Holland

FSC
Mixed Sources
Product group from well-managed
forests and other controlled sources

Cert no. SW-COC-002283
www.fsc.org
© 1996 Forest Stewardship Council

ISBN: 978-1-934759-31-8
      1-934759-31-7

Library of Congress Control Number: 2009928229

Manufactured, Typeset, and Printed in the United States of America

DEDICATIONS

To my wife, Hannah, who has been at my side for more than three decades; my daughter, Stefanie, and her husband, Nathan; my daughter, Madeline; and the rest of my family. None of what I do would matter very much if they were not in my life.

Acknowledgments

There is no way I can claim to have invented the simple but powerful lessons of this book. They come from a lifetime of working with professionals, entrepreneurs, and small business owners—as their coach, as their sales trainer, and as their colleague.

Most of the conversations I relate on the pages that follow took place verbatim. Names were changed to avoid anyone embarrassment, but some of my clients and associates who have seen these pages have immediately recognized themselves.

Without their challenges and questions, many of the lessons would not have made their way onto these pages, and I want to acknowledge their important contributions.

The subscribers to my Blog and e-letter are due an acknowledgment, too. They kept me thinking and writing about the topic of getting and keeping quality clients. They also kept reminding me to put in writing the ideas I gleaned from my interactions with them that could be used to help others.

My wife, Hannah, is owed an acknowledgment, not just for allowing me the time to do the writing, but for bringing me questions from her sales experience that have made their way into this book.

I acknowledge my coach, Steve Chandler, for seeing instantly what I was trying to convey in this book... and encouraging me to get it published.

Finally, I owe a debt of gratitude to the managers and representatives of the financial firm that I have been working with for more than ten years, who I choose to leave anonymous, lest they be connected with me in some way over which they have no control. They have been instrumental in allowing me to test the many ideas that go onto these pages; so that I can say, with certainty, that even in the aftermath of a vicious economic downturn, if you take the simple steps I give you here, you'll find more clients and better clients and you'll keep your clients longer.

Sandy Schussel
Princeton, New Jersey
March, 2009

FOREWORD

A Perfect Manual for the Times We Live In

Often we hear about some new book possessing a "timeless" wisdom. What I like about Sandy Schussel's book on professional service selling is that it is *not* timeless. It's the opposite: it's a book especially written for these times we are in.

This book is timely in two important ways: First, it is written in brief, impactful sound bites. In today's world of texting and Twittering and two-sentence emails, a book like this fits right in. It's quick and easy to read. It doesn't waste the time or overload the bandwidth of a busy, multi-tasking reader.

Thank you!

The second way this book is timely is that it is the perfect frugal, powerful antidote to the recession. It offers sales tools and techniques that require no bloating of the budget. Rather, the opposite. It returns the professional to the best possible practices of relationship building.

Sandy's background as an attorney shows through in his sensitivity to the issue of selling under the radar. There are no crass or overt "selling" techniques that professionals understandably recoil from. His short segments on creative listening and attraction-versus-promotion allow his readers to become master "sales and marketing" practitioners, without any pushy components or hucksterism.

America's professional firms have, in a way, been on a vacation from history. They have had the financial luxury of riding booms in real estate combined with access to seemingly unlimited credit lines. During that period of time, there was less need to learn to be artful at selling.

But the winds have shifted, and professionals are now faced with a choice. They can hunker down and board up the windows, lay people off, and hope the hurricane passes. Or they can change the way they obtain clients. They can hide out, or use the economy as a reason to learn to sell.

Those professionals who simply cut expenses, lay people off, and hide under the blankets "till it's over" will grow weaker and even less likely to survive.

But those who take this little book in their hands and use it as a flight manual will be able to create their own future. They will learn to fly.

The great novelist Robert Louis Stevenson once said, "Everyone lives by selling something." The problem is that many people realize this fact a bit too late. Sandy Schussel's book is a way to wake up in time. And to realize that as long as this enterprise system we live in remains free, selling will always be what best determines success.

Many of the prescriptions in this book are wonderfully counter-intuitive. All of our aversions to what we assume selling must be—aggressive "cold calling" and "closing techniques"—are set to rest. The prescriptions here require none of the old strong-arm approaches, and focus more on gentle inquiries, listening skills, and graceful and enjoyable approaches that any of us can immediately put into practice.

It's ironic that the very thing that would save professional firms from economic trouble is the same thing they have had the most aversion to—until now. With this useful guide, any professional can become a master at determining his own destiny through sales skill.

Steve Chandler
Phoenix, Arizona
March, 2009

Table of Contents

Part 4
Dos and Don'ts

Part 5
It's Easy... Just Do It!

INTRODUCTION

What if the economy was always booming and there were more clients to go around for every professional than there were professionals to meet their needs?

What if in order to make senior partner in your firm, you didn't have to bring in any clients?

What if the question of having accounts of your own to bring with you was never asked on a professional job interview?

What if business never got slow, or if it did get slow, you could just do the services you were trained to do and are good at, and more people would just come to you? Like the Pied Piper, you'd start to play your flute and clients would follow you wherever you go?

Now, let's get real!

Even medical professionals who can rely upon third-party reimbursement run into periods when not enough patients are coming through their doors. Few professionals are immune to difficult economic periods and competition. Another thing most of them have in common is that they dread the thought of having to commit "S & M"—that is, Sales and Marketing.

"If I wanted to be in sales," an engineer client told me, "I would not have studied engineering." So, when there's not enough engineering work, he and his partners work on their files, overwork existing projects, and develop plans for clients of the future. But they don't go out and do the work they most need to do—get more clients.

The pages that follow were written with those engineers in mind, along with the lawyers, accountants, coaches, chiropractors, dentists, doctors, complimentary medical specialists, graphic artists, and consultants of every kind who are either afraid of sales and marketing, or don't know how to do it in a way that allows them to continue to feel dignified and professional.

This book is intended to be quick, interesting, and sometimes humorous, with some simple but important lessons about growing a professional practice in any economic or competitive environment. The lessons are easy to implement, generally don't cost anything, and will have an immediate and powerful impact on your practice or business, no matter what the economy is doing.

Jump in now, and start applying the lessons as you learn them. You'll be glad you did.

Part 1: Who Are You and Why Should I Buy What You Have to Offer?

HERE I'M MESMERIZED AGAIN. YOU'RE A BOLD AND RAVISHING RED CRAYON.

Jo Davidson
Singer/Songwriter

ONE

Be The RED CRAYON

Crayon

For those of us who are selling professional services of one kind or another, our "next level" is getting more clients (or patients), getting better clients, or simply keeping the clients we have already.

Many of us are stuck in a mindset—a paradigm—that the only way we can grow is to do something we dread: marketing, "prospecting," or (horror of horrors) selling.

"But I'm an engineer," my client Ted protested, *"not a SALESMAN."*

The picture Ted had in his mind of someone who sells his services is the pushy salesman on the used car lot with the loud plaid sports jacket, the phony smile, and the bad toupee. Who wants to be *that* guy? Even most used car salesmen don't want to be that guy.

Like most of my clients, Ted couldn't fill his day with work for quality clients for two reasons:

1. He didn't know how to attract more business.

2. He was afraid of cold calling, making presentations, and other "sales" things he was sure I'd be making him do.

"What if instead of marketing, prospecting, and selling, you just *positioned yourself* to attract the clients you want?" I asked Ted.

"I don't know what you mean," he responded, "but that sounds a lot better than selling."

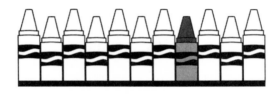

If you're just another financial advisor, cleaning service operator, or dentist, you're faced with competition from dozens—or hundreds—of people doing the same work. You're another white crayon in a box filled with white crayons. You will get business, but your ability to get more and better clients and patients will be limited. Sending out mailings or refrigerator magnets, making cold calls, and other marketing and sales activities might pull in the occasional new client, but what will work faster and better is having a way to distinguish yourself from all of the other white crayons.

Instead of struggling to sell your services, position yourself as the one red crayon in the box, as a provider who can fulfill a specific need for a specific type of client.

Every day I speak to professionals and salespeople who are telling people they are brokers, or lawyers, or coaches, or web designers, or IT professionals, without differentiating themselves from all of the other people who do "the same thing." Each of them is just one more white crayon in a box of white crayons.

The point they miss is that clients are more attracted to experts and specialists—or someone unique—than they are to general practitioners who look like all the other general practitioners in any field. Your prospective clients and patients are looking for the red crayon. Start attracting them by giving them what they're looking for.

I recently spoke with a chiropractor who protested that he couldn't be a red crayon. He was "just another chiropractor." When I "Googled" him before our call, I had found an article about using cold laser applications for relief of pain in which he had been quoted as an experienced cold laser practitioner.

I told him his expertise in this field was already a way he could attract patients. But as we spoke, he mentioned a recent experience with Reiki healing that had made him feel that he had become better with his hands at doing chiropractic manipulation than he had ever been.

There were now two powerful distinctions that made this professional the red crayon in his particular box of white crayons, which could, if properly utilized, attract many more new patients to him than any "sales" effort he could ever mount.

So why did he choose to be just another chiropractor? Like many of us, he was afraid to be the red crayon.

If you recognize that what holds you back is fear of standing out, try to rise above that fear. Get help with it. Be the red crayon. It will bring you more clients and more job offers with less selling.

TWO

IF YOU CAN, BE FIRST. IF YOU CAN'T BE FIRST, CREATE A NEW CATEGORY IN WHICH YOU CAN BE FIRST.

Al Ries and Jack Trout,
The 22 Immutable Laws of Marketing

"Can you hear me now?"

"Branding" is a primary way to attract business. It is an expression of your identity through various strategies you use to create the perception that your services are the *only* solution to someone's problems. If you're in a practice or a business—even if you're just on the job market occasionally— you need to know something about branding.

It's not simply about showing how you're different from your competitors. It's about having your clients or prospects believe that what you offer is exactly the solution they need.

If I meet someone at a party or gathering, tell him during our conversation that I'm a great coach for anyone who sells a service, and ask him if he would like to work with me, I'm engaging in direct marketing.

If, instead, that person comes across the room and says to me, "I hear that you're a great coach for anyone who sells a service, and I'd like to work with you," I've successfully branded my business.

To brand yourself and your work, you need to take three preliminary steps:

1. **Select a Target Market.** Who do you most want to work with or for? As a professional, a consultant, or a service-business owner, you will have more success if you become an expert in the needs of one particular narrow target market: Teenagers, "Boomers," families, entrepreneurs, landscaping contractors, retirees, ADD adults, etc. It's aiming a high-powered rifle with a laser scope at selected targets in a range full of them—scoring a bulls  eye almost every time—rather than shooting out hundreds of pounds of buckshot in the general direction of the targets in the hope of hitting something.

2. **Identify one to three "core needs."** What are your clients' biggest problems or needs? Obviously, you want to talk about the needs that you have solutions for. Your typical client may need dental work, but if you have a house cleaning service, this isn't a core need you can use.

3. **Design your unique solutions.** Why will people or businesses in your target market buy the services they need from you and not your competitors? Clients like "packages." If the solutions you provide are not unique, start thinking about ways to package them to make them unique. If you're just another white crayon in a box of white crayons, there's no good reason to use your services. Be the red crayon in the box.

In 1994, in *The 22 Immutable Laws of Marketing*, Al Ries and Jack Trout wrote: "If you can, be first. If you can't be first, create a new category in which you can be first." FedEx is the one to use "when it absolutely, positively has to be there over night." When are *you* the one to utilize?

YOUR AD IS THERE TO REACH SOMEONE.

IT MUST REACH SOMEONE.

IF IT DOESN'T REACH SOMEONE THE VERY FIRST TIME, IT IS A WASTE OF MONEY.

Steve Chandler and Sam Beckford
9 Lies That Are Holding Your Business Back

Keep Your Picture SIMPLE

When my daughters were little, I used to love to read a book to them that appears now to be out of print; *Simple Pictures Are Best*, by Nancy Willard.

It was a story of a farmer and his wife who decided to buy each other a session with a professional photographer for their anniversary. The fun begins when the photographer comes and the couple can't decide what to wear, where to sit, or what to include in the picture. The farmer ends up wearing his new shoes on his feet while showing off his old shoes on his ears with arms full of farm produce. His wife wears both of her hats, and brings out all of her pets, and her kitchen and gardening utensils.

Each time the couple decides to add something to their picture, the photographer warns, "Simple pictures are best." But  the couple continues to ignore him and assembles everything they can think of for the photograph. Finally, the commotion causes the farmer's bull to charge at the photographer, and the only picture taken that day is of the bull.

Recently, I worked with Ryan, a client whose company provides computer graphics services to financial services businesses. Ryan was running two huge, expensive half-page ads weekly in a local paper with a broad-based, mostly-business readership.

"How much business do these ads generate?" I asked him.

"I don't know," was his reply.

It turned out that he had been running these ads for years, spending hundreds of thousands of dollars over time, but had never asked his new clients how they found out about his company, and had never asked existing clients whether they had even seen the ads.

"If you don't know whether there's any benefit to running these ads," I asked him, "Why do you keep running them?"

His answer took several minutes. He told me about how he started these ad campaigns along with several other very broad marketing efforts years before. He also disclosed that he was still paying for a lot of other advertising and marketing efforts without knowing whether they were working or not.

I thought of the farmer with the shoes on his ears and his feet, and arms full of produce.

"Simple pictures are best," I said to Ryan.

Scientists will tell you about Occam's Razor, a theory that essentially says, "All things being equal, the simplest of all possible solutions is the best." Used another way, it tells us that when there are several possible explanations for something, the simplest explanation is probably the right one.

The "simple pictures" rule tells us that if you have a business or practice and are looking to market it, the simplest marketing picture is probably the best:

1. Be very clear about who your target is.

2. Choose strategies that are designed to reach that very clear target.

3. Test to see whether and to what extent those strategies are working.

4. Keep using the ones that work until you have the kind of business or practice that you want.

27

IF YOU DON'T KNOW WHO OR WHERE YOUR IDEAL CLIENTS ARE, YOU WON'T KNOW WHERE TO NETWORK OR SPEAK OR MAIL.

Robert Middleton
Infoguru Manual

FOUR

To whom are you offering/selling your services?

The wrong answer to this question is "I offer my services to everyone." Lawyers who tell me they are general practitioners; financial advisors and coaches who tell me that they help (all) people reach (all of) their personal, career, or financial goals; and entrepreneurs who tell me that just about anyone can use their services do not understand a critical truth about Twenty-first Century business—clients want to work with experts and specialists.

If I want a lawyer to handle a real estate matter, and the cost isn't significantly different, would I prefer a "real estate specialist" or a generic lawyer who happens to do real estate? The answer should be obvious. Both attorneys may have the same training and background—they may even have the same experience in real estate—but one has narrowed his target and focus to make himself more appealing.

"But if I limit myself to my senior market," Tina, a financial advisor, complained when I introduced this concept at a recent seminar, "I'll turn off some younger people who might have wanted to use my services."

Limit Your Target, Not Your Services

I asked Tina to trust in what I was saying and to try it. A week later she called me, excited by her results. "Sandy, I tried what you suggested at a party last week and it worked, but I think it worked backwards," she exclaimed.

> "I told a guy who was in his mid-thirties like I am that I help older, single women who are worried about whether they'll have enough money to last through their retirement years... and he asked me if I would make an exception to help him."

I didn't know what to say," Tina continued, "so I told him I would work with him, but only if he was very serious about his retirement."

"He said he was," Tina concluded, "and now I have an appointment with him next week."

"Tina, that isn't backwards," I assured her. "That's how it works."

Being a specialist not only attracts your ideal client, it actually attracts people from other walks of life as well. I offer my assistance to people selling a service who want more clients. When someone who does not fit my marketing profile asks for my help, I only refuse him or her if I think there may be someone who will do a better job.

So, along with owners of service businesses and their sales and marketing teams, I'm coaching executives who are climbing the corporate ladder and IT professionals who are looking for a permanent position. I'm even working with an entertainer who is breaking into her newly chosen field after a first career. I'm an expert in the problems of people who are struggling to grow their businesses or practices, but I'll help anyone who is serious about making his or her life or career better.

When someone asks, *"What do YOU do?"* Don't be afraid to identify your favorite clients or work. It will help make you stand out from the crowd.

WE DELIVER HOT, FRESH PIZZA IN 30 MINUTES OR LESS OR IT'S FREE.

Domino's Pizza

FIVE

Know Why I Should Buy it From YOU

You might be thinking that you don't "sell" services and people don't "buy" them. Maybe someone "retains" or "consults" you and you "provide" your services. But if we're being completely honest, someone is selling and someone is buying. Here are the three universal things anyone selling his or her services needs to know:

What are you selling or offering?

To whom are you selling or offering it?

Why should they buy it from/hire you?

The third point—the "why"—seems to be the one that gives some people the most trouble.

"You should work with me because I really care about my clients," Terry, a two-year veteran financial advisor posed in role-play with me.

"But that's exactly what [your competitor] said to me," I responded. "Why should I choose you over him?"

Terry was stumped. "If we're all apples on a supermarket shelf," I asked him, "what difference does it make which apple I pick? All of them would tell me, if they could talk, that they are red, sweet, and juicy."

Once again, Terry had no answer.

"What is different about you," I asked him again, "from all the other people who do what you do?"

"Well, I'm not really different in any way" he started; "we all provide the same kinds of planning services, and give advice aimed at the same goals… I just know I would be more caring than anyone else."

"What makes you think so?" I pressed.

Terry thought for a moment and then responded hesitantly:

"My father died when I was just a teenager and left us with no money, so I know how important having money is, and I made up my mind that I would spend my life helping people prevent that from happening to their families."

As soon as the words were out of his mouth, Terry's face brightened. He realized he had stumbled on the perfect answer, for him, to the "why you" question.

When you can tell people why they should hire you or use your services in a way that distinguishes you from the other sweet, juicy red apples, you'll get more business.

Part 2: Attract the Clients You Really Want

YOU ARE THE MOST POWERFUL MAGNET IN THE UNIVERSE! YOU CONTAIN A MAGNETIC POWER WITHIN YOU THAT IS MORE POWERFUL THAN ANYTHING IN THIS WORLD, AND THIS UNFATHOMABLE MAGNETIC POWER IS EMITTED THROUGH YOUR THOUGHTS.

Rhonda Byrne

ATTRACT
Clients; Don't Pursue Them

SIX

Devon, an engineer, was complaining that he did not have time to sit down and think about the ad he wanted to run in the local newspaper. He was looking for small design jobs he could do as a side business. He had done several of these jobs, but the economy had caused this work to dry up for him.

"Don't bother with it then," I told him.

"What do you mean?" he asked incredulously, "I *have* to advertise."

"Maybe that's true," I responded. "You can *pursue* clients through advertising any time. Why don't you try *attracting* them first?"

While there are many methods a professional might use to grow his or her client base, they usually fall into one of two categories: methods that *attract* clients and methods that involve *pursuing* them. Both work, but attracting clients usually costs a lot less and ends up being a lot more effective and rewarding.

When you are *attracting* clients, you draw them to you in a natural, comfortable, professional way. Your efforts might include any or all of the following:

~ Dazzling existing clients with service so spectacular that they talk about you in a positive way with everyone they know:

> *"Do you know what my attorney did last night?"*

~ Meeting people through introductions from clients and others who already know you

~ Getting out where your target clients congregate and being with them

~ Becoming a recognized expert through articles, books, and appearances

Pursuing clients, by contrast, involves spending time and money on more traditional efforts such as advertising, cold calling, e-mail blasts, or direct mail. One client doesn't necessarily lead to another, which means the effort needs to be repeated over and over again, generating ever more effort and expense.

A related challenge is that when people hear an advertising message several times, they stop hearing it altogether. This means that the message has to be changed over and over again, resulting in more expense. But if you stop your pursuit, the flow of prospects stops, also.

If you are selling professional services of any kind, there's a good chance that attracting clients will be the more effective approach for you. To get attraction methods to work, you need to: (1) be professionally attractive and (2) find connections to your target.

Being professionally attractive. No, I don't mean you have to be good looking; but you do have to dress, act, speak, and appear to your chosen target the way they would expect a professional of your caliber to appear.

Some traits are universally attractive: personal integrity, having a life purpose, and passion. People want to be around a person who is clear about who he or she is, and about what matters to him or her. Such a person is often viewed as a leader.

If you want to be professionally attractive, start with these traits and then make sure the image you project—your "outward" appearance—is one that matches your clients' expectations.

Finding connections to your target. Don't sit in your office waiting for the phone to ring. Get out and interact with your prospective clients. Get introduced to them, go where they go, talk to them, and write articles (and books) for them to read. In most professions, people want to experience you as a person, not just as a professional, before they commit to you. Create those opportunities for yourself.

Before you spend a fortune on pursuing clients, try attracting them. Devon started calling his existing clients to talk about the value he provided them, and to ask if they knew people who needed the same kind of work done. He was amazed to find that several of his clients were happy to arrange introductions to other people who had seen his work and who had an interest in having the same thing done for them.

SEVEN

Don't Keep Who You WANT to Work with a Secret

YES. SHRUBBERIES ARE MY TRADE. I AM A SHRUBBER. MY NAME IS ROGER THE SHRUBBER. I ARRANGE, DESIGN, AND SELL SHRUBBERIES.

Monty Python

"It appears that you've already got nearly as many clients as you can handle," I declared to Victoria, a CPA (Certified Public Accountant) who had just started working with me. "How can I help you?"

"None of them have any money," she confided.

Victoria is 27 years old. She has managed to grow her accounting practice to its current level by giving terrific service to small retailers, most of whom are young and either just starting out or have been in business less than two years.

These clients are often struggling and can barely afford basic accounting services. Invariably, her happy clients recommend Victoria to their young entrepreneur friends. While she is grateful for their loyalty, she is frustrated about starting to work with still more struggling small business owners.

I explained to Victoria that you can't attract what you want into your life—clients or anything else—unless you have a clear picture of whatever it is that you can share with people.

"It's hard for you to make the kind of living you want on these small clients," I acknowledged, "so then, who do you *want* to take on as a client?" I asked her.

Victoria thought a moment, and then replied, "Well, I do like to work with 'Mom and Pop' business owners, but I wish I could be working with some that are larger and more established."

"Then tell your clients that's who you're looking for," I challenged her.

"Just like that?" she asked. "I don't know...."

Two days later, Victoria called. With excitement rushing her words, she related the details of her conversation with one of her small business owners, a new independent copy store:

44

"I was finishing up the paperwork with Tom, the owner, when he told me he had recommended me to a friend of his who had just opened a small deli. I thanked him for the referral, but then I did what you told me to do. I said 'Tom, you know I always appreciate your faith in me, and I will always take good care of anyone you recommend me to; but I do my best work with people who have larger, more established businesses.' Tom's wife, Marie, happened to be walking by while I was saying this and said, 'Why don't we send her to see my uncle?'"

Then, Victoria told me the outcome: "Marie's uncle owns a large, well-known furniture store in the next town. I have an appointment to see him next week."

What kind of client can I get for you today?

Victoria's accounts knew she wanted more clients, but they thought she wanted more clients like them. Victoria learned that people don't know what you want until you tell them, and asking for what she wanted resulted in her landing exactly the kind of client she was hoping to reach.

FOLLOW UP! FOLLOW UP! FOLLOW UP! THIS IS THE KEY TO BUILDING RELATIONSHIPS WITH OTHERS.

Joy Weaver

YOU'RE NOT BUGGING ME IF YOU KNOW YOU CAN SOLVE MY HEADACHE.

Diane Darling

Follow Up, Follow Up, Follow UP!

EIGHT

You met someone at a party who is in a position where she might be able to use your services. You had the *"What do YOU do?"* conversation, and you exchanged business cards.

If she's interested in learning more about your services and how you might help her, you can just assume she'll call you, right? I mean, if you contact her to try to learn more about her situation and tell her more about your services, she'll think you're needy or pushy or have some ulterior motive, won't she?

So, you don't try to approach her and, although you hoped she was impressed and interested, she doesn't call.

We give ourselves many reasons for not following-up with the people we meet. We tell ourselves:

~ If they're interested, they'll contact me.

~ If I contact them, I'll be seen as pushy.

~ If I contact them, they'll think I'm desperate for business.

~ I have more immediate and more important things to do.

But all of these "reasons" are the work of the *"But" Monster* I talk about in my book, *The High Diving Board*—they're simply excuses you make because you're afraid of being rejected.

Let's look at these excuses more closely:

If they're interested, they'll contact me. On occasion, this *does* happen, but maybe they've misplaced your card and forgotten your last name, or simply got busy with their own work. If it seemed as if they were interested, shouldn't you contact them to be sure?

If I contact them, I'll be seen as pushy. If you're pushy, you'll be seen as pushy. The contact is just a way of asking if they'd like to continue your dialogue.

If I contact them, they'll think I'm desperate for business. Most people view a follow-up contact as an expected business practice. They may or may not be receptive to it, but they will not see it as needy unless you make it appear that way.

I have more immediate and more important things to do. How many of the things that you're doing are more important than bringing in new clients?

Follow-up contact works best when you do it right away, and it's *easy*. You can choose from among making a phone call, which is the most effective way; sending a hand-written note, which is viewed as special and personal but involves a precious time loss waiting for delivery; and e-mailing, which is not as personal, but can be done instantaneously, the next day or over the weekend.

Here's an example of an e-mail or hand-written follow-up note:

> *Tom,*
>
> *It was a pleasure meeting you at Pete's party Friday night. You mentioned your son was sick. I hope he's feeling better. I had the sense from what you told me about your situation that I might be able to help. If you'd like to get together, so I can learn a little bit more, let me know.*
>
> *Either way, though, I hope our paths cross again.*
>
> *—Sandy Schussel*

A follow-up phone call might sound something like this:

> *Hi, Tom! This is Sandy Schussel. We met at Pete's party last Friday... I had the sense from what you told me about your situation, that I might be able to help you. We could talk now on the phone if this is a good time or, if you'd prefer, we could set up a time to get together in person and talk. What are your thoughts?*

49

Follow-up contacts — especially phone calls — open opportunities you might never have anticipated. Create a mindset that follow-up contact is one of your most important jobs and that it can help you grow your business.

Part 3: How to "Sell" as a Professional

WHEN YOU ASK QUESTIONS
TO GET CLIENTS TALKING
ABOUT THEIR NEEDS,
YOU'RE SELLING;
YOU'RE FINDING OUT WHAT
THEY WANT TO OWN.
ONLY THEN CAN YOU
GUIDE THEM TO THE
RIGHT PRODUCT OR SERVICE.

Tom Hopkins

Reframe Your View of the "S" Word

NINE

Now, I'd like to talk about the *other end* of the client funnel—the one involving the "S" word. You know...*sales*. Whether you're a professional selling your services, trying to get a job, or looking for a business partner, at some point, you'll be selling.

But if that thought scares you, take heart. It's easier than you think. Selling isn't what you may think it is. It's not about coming up with a powerful presentation, and compelling or manipulating someone to buy something you offer.

Selling is the asking of appropriate questions so that your prospective client determines for himself or herself that he or she needs what you offer.

Anything you can *tell* a client or prospective client, you can *get them to tell you*, if you ask the right questions.

Contrary to what many of the great sales "gurus" of the Twentieth Century were preaching, "closing" a sale is usually the least important part of the sales process. Sure, you have to ask them if they're willing to take the final step, but like the rest of the process, closing is accomplished simply by asking a question:

"So, should we get started?"

"What do you think the next step is?"

"When would you like to start?"

Nor is the important part of the sale a *presentation*. Yes, you need to explain your solution to a prospect's problem, but this can best be done as a *conversation*.

Selling happens when you **ask powerful questions**—questions about consequences, and questions that elicit emotions and unearth an explicit need or problem. Ask questions that elicit emotions and you'll convince them early in your conversation that they should be working with you:

"How do you feel about that?"

"Is it important?"

"What's important about it to you?"

"If we can fix that, how will that affect you in the long run?"

"How would you feel then?"

Only when your questions have uncovered a need or desire—
and they usually will if you take your time—should you be
talking about your solutions. When you do, your conversation
should be about the solutions that address their very specific
need or desire. Then you can ask for the "sale."

Stop worrying about *selling*, and turn more of your possibles
into definites by asking more and better questions.

FIND OUT
WHO YOU ARE
AND DO IT ON PURPOSE.

Dolly Parton

TEN

If You WANT More Clients, Do It On purpose

"Before we discuss whether we're all in sales," I asked at a recent workshop of assorted professionals, "someone tell me what *selling* is?"

"Getting people to buy what you're offering," one attendee answered.

"Manipulating them into doing what you want them to do," volunteered another.

"Twisting their words around so they feel like they're foolish if they don't use your services," proclaimed another.

After hearing a few more negative descriptions like these, I asked them to try on the definition I used in the last chapter:

Selling is the asking of appropriate questions so that your prospective client determines for himself or herself that he or she needs what you offer.

The room was suddenly quiet. So I asked six questions:

1. Do you ask questions?

2. Do you listen carefully to the answers—maybe even write them down and think about them?

3. Do those questions lead to more questions?

4. Do you make recommendations?

5. Do you give examples of how what you do might work?

6. Do they conclude for themselves that they need your services?

Observing that virtually all of them had been nodding their heads in the affirmative after every question, I proclaimed: "Then, you are all used to selling. Now, I want to talk to you about doing it on purpose."

Maybe you want more clients or better clients, but you're one of those professionals who views sales as something the guy in the plaid jacket and bad hairpiece does. You picture him with a big phony smile, on the used car lot, telling fibs about the history of the clunker he's trying to sell you, and pretending to bring your offer to his manager. If this is your thinking when we talk about selling, then the first thing you need to do is to change your paradigm.

If you have *any* customers, clients, or patients at all, you've been selling. If you start observing carefully what you do right, and then duplicate it, you'll get more and better customers, clients, or patients.

IF I HAD EIGHT HOURS TO CHOP DOWN A TREE, I'D SPEND SIX SHARPENING MY AXE.

Abraham Lincoln

Learn the Basic Sales Skills for Professionals

ELEVEN

As you may have surmised by now, I view asking questions as an important sales skill. To be truly successful at getting clients, your passion for your firm's work must, actually, be accompanied by mastery of *three* skills:

1. The ability to ask powerful, provocative questions

2. The ability to listen with total focus on the client

3. The ability to relate moving stories and metaphors

While I've already devoted a good deal of attention to the first of these skills, **the ability to ask powerful, provocative questions,** I believe so strongly that it is the most important skill that I bring it up here again.

If you've found your prospective client (we'll call him or her a "prospect") backing away, it is likely that you have made the common mistake of cutting the questioning process short. You may have jumped to the solution you provide too early.

If you're like most professionals, before talking about your services, you ask informational questions—who, what, where, when, how, and why. While you need this information to understand how you can help your prospect, it is more valuable to you than it is to him or her. The prospect already has this information.

Sometimes, your informational questions bring up a need, concern, or problem—maybe even one that the prospect didn't know he or she had. Maybe the prospect is working with someone in your field and is having some problems with the relationship or the results he is getting.

Well, that's what you do, isn't it? You solve problems. And there they are.

As soon as you identify this little bit of trouble in Paradise, you pounce with your solution...and the prospect starts squirming and backing away.

Here's an example of a conversation my client, Lisa, a financial advisor, had with a prospect who had been working with another advisor:

Lisa: *So you haven't heard from him in over a year, and he didn't return your call the last time you tried to reach him? He also hasn't explained any of these things we've been talking about today, right? It sounds like you're not getting the service you need from him. I can promise you that I'll check in with you once a quarter, and I return my calls immediately. How about if we transfer these accounts?*

Prospect: *No. I've been working with him for eight years. I think I'll try to talk to him again first, and if he doesn't return my call, I'll get back to you.*

The reason this conversation ended as it did is that the problem Lisa identified is an *implied* one. Your prospects are always weighing whether their need for a change is explicit and urgent enough that it is worth their while to go through the fuss and bother of moving their accounts or changing their providers.

When there's only a vague sense of a problem, the scale tips in favor of leaving things as they are. To avoid running into a brick wall, you need to move from implied problems to *explicit* problems. You get your prospects to see the explicit need by asking provocative questions.

Here's how Lisa might sound after learning to ask better questions:

Lisa: *So you haven't heard from him in over a year, and he didn't return your call the last time you tried to reach him? He also hasn't explained any of these things we've been talking about today, right? How is this level of service affecting you?*

Prospect: *It's a little annoying that he can't return my call, but I guess I'm doing okay.*

Lisa: *Does it concern you that there's no one reassuring you about your retirement or explaining these things to you?*

Prospect: *Well, actually, that's the reason I agreed to sit down with you. I am concerned that there might be more I should be doing or that I need to change my strategy.*

Lisa: *And if you continue to get no service or you try him again, and maybe he responds this time, but doesn't respond next time, will you be okay with that?*

Prospect: *Well, no. I need to feel that someone is watching out for me. Maybe my account is just too small for him.*

Lisa: *What's at stake here?*

Prospect: *This is my life savings we're talking about!*

Lisa: *Yes, it is your life savings. Does it make more sense to you to wait and see—and worry about it all the time—or to try working with someone who is promising to be there for you?*

Prospect: *I really shouldn't wait for it to happen again. Tell me about how you work . . .*

Don't jump in with solutions until you've asked enough good questions to move your prospect from an implied need to an explicit need. To get more clients, ask powerful, provocative questions.

Now, let's take a look at the second of the three sales skills:

The ability to listen with total focus on the client.

Anyone who is married knows that we really don't listen to each other. I could call my wife, Hannah, from my office and say something like:

"Honey, you won't believe this! I got to work fifteen minutes late this morning and when I looked out the window there was a flying saucer with two little green men in it. They waved and flew off into space . . ."

Hannah would then probably ask:

"Why were you late? You left on time."

65

Many of us are trying to listen to one another, text messaging, and watching television all at the same time. When we are doing all of these things at once, the listening part of this multitasking is *passive* listening.

Some of my clients and friends have taken courses on *active* listening. They've been told:

"When you're speaking with a client, stop everything else, put your papers aside, turn away from the computer, make eye contact with the client, concentrate on the words he is speaking, and don't interrupt."

These are all important, but they still don't protect us from one of the biggest stumbling blocks to listening with total focus: Being "Waiting to Talk" listeners. Even when we stop all activity and elect to listen actively, our minds may be racing through responses for whatever it is that the client or prospect is saying. So, often we miss the most important component of communication—the emotion behind the words.

Listening with *total focus on the client* requires all of the skills you need for active listening, but adds the requirement that you let go of the need to hunt for a response. Listen to the words, listen for the emotions behind the words, and observe the client's body language. Listen for what they are saying, but also for what they're not saying.

Professionals who are totally focused on their clients and prospects when they are listening to them are always more likely to win—or keep—them as clients. But it's not easy to do this right. It will take practice, and maybe some coaching.

Now, let's discuss the third skill:

The ability to relate moving stories and metaphors.

Testimonials about your service help you get clients because humans are hard-wired to pay attention to, focus on, and respond to stories. As societies developed through the centuries, telling stories around a campfire became commonplace. This tradition gave way to fireplace stories. Books and publications brought stories in writing; and radio, television and computers kept the tradition going.

When there are no clients around to tell their story about your service, however—or campfires, for that matter—your own stories of your exploits can assist you to turn an uncertain prospect into a ready client.

Stories—metaphors, illustrations, etc.—are important everywhere in the process of selling services.

My client Michael, an attorney, is a master at "sales" stories:

> "Joe, your situation is very similar to the situation of a client I'm helping at the moment. He had a little more money invested than you do in his piece of real estate, but what the seller did in his case was almost identical to what happened to you. Just like you, he struggled with whether he should spend the money on starting litigation or not; but he decided he couldn't let them get away with it and asked me to go ahead with it."

It's a rare instance when a prospective client doesn't yield in the face of stories like these.

Michael also uses metaphors. I remember our discussion about a client with a small case who asked Michael whether or not she could handle it herself – without a lawyer.

"Sure you can," Michael told her, "But then you'd be like a leaf on a rushing stream. With no rudder and no one to steer, you'd be rushing toward whatever result the system intends for you."

The woman took out her checkbook and wrote a retainer check.

One of my favorite masters of metaphor was Ben Feldman, one of the greatest insurance salesmen in modern history. Ben could look prospective insurance purchasers in the eyes and say things like, "With the stroke of a pen, you create an estate," and the prospects would pick up their pens to sign the application Ben brought with him.

Another client of mine, Larry, is a financial advisor. To explain a Roth IRA, where you invest with after-tax dollars into an account that can grow income tax-free if held long enough, Larry uses a farming metaphor:

"If you were a farmer and you had to pay taxes," he asks, "would you rather pay taxes on the seed, or on the crop that you harvest?"

"The seed, I guess," is the prospect's reply.

"Why is that?" Larry asks.

"Well, I'm sure the seed is valuable, but I imagine that the crop will bring a lot more money when they harvest it, and the tax on that will be much higher."

"I think you're right," Larry agrees. "Do you see how that relates to this investment?" he asks. "You'll already have paid the taxes on the seed—the money you put in at the beginning—and you'll be able to harvest the crop tax-free."

In case you missed it, Larry manages to put all three skills together in his conversation. He asks provocative questions, listens carefully to the answer, and uses a metaphor that allows his prospect to make the right choice.

These three skills will help you get more clients, get better clients, and keep the clients you have for much longer.

YOU CAN CLOSE MORE BUSINESS IN TWO MONTHS BY BECOMING INTERESTED IN OTHER PEOPLE THAN YOU CAN IN TWO YEARS BY TRYING TO GET PEOPLE INTERESTED IN YOU.

Dale Carnegie

Be Impressed, Not Impressive

TWELVE

(Lessons From The Master, Part I)

"Master?" The young professional addressed his mentor. "You have told us that in order to hire us, a client must Like us and Trust us."

"That is correct, Grasshopper," the Master replied.

"I understand how I can earn a client's Trust," continued the Young Professional, "But how do I get him to like me in the short time I might be in his presence?"

The other Professionals snickered at this simple question, but they were secretly glad their classmate was so bold as to ask it, because they did not know the answer, either.

The Master smiled gently and explained, "To be liked, you must try to stop being liked."

A look of confusion passed across the students' faces, and although he was blind, the Master could see it.

"We want to talk about our education, our skills, and our accomplishments. We want our clients to see how well we

71

dress, and the fine vehicles and homes we have acquired through our efforts. We want them to warm to our smiles and our conversation," the Master explained, "but what our clients want is for us to like them."

 "To be liked by a client, Grasshopper," the Master continued, "the client must perceive that you like him—that you are impressed with his accomplishments, however small they might be, and that you care about him."

"Ah," exclaimed the younger man, "I must be impressed, rather than impressive."

"Good, Grasshopper," the Master said, gently smiling. "But it's more than being impressed," he continued, "You must... Listen deeply, and ask questions with Childlike Curiosity— not just about the problem you were trained to solve, but about his family, his hopes, and his dreams."

A light began to grow in the younger man's eyes and, once again, the blind Master could see it.

"What you seem to be saying, Master," he began with excitement in his voice, "is that clients don't care how much we know, until they know how much we care. Is that it?"

"Yes, Grasshopper," the Master replied warmly, "You have learned well."

The younger man bowed, and the blind Master acknowledged it.

THIRTEEN

Bring the FOUR Swordsmen of Client SERVICE with You

WHAT CLIENTS WANT:

RESPECT

+EMPATHY

+ACTION

+COMMUNICATION

TRUST

(Lessons From The Master, Part II)

"Grasshopper," the Master called to the Young Professional, seeming to stare right at him, "last time we spoke you told me you knew how to build Trust with a Client, and I did not challenge you. Now, I must ask," the Master continued, "How *does* one build Trust with a Client?"

The Young Professional did not hesitate with his response. "Master," he replied, "you have already taught me that Trust comes with the Four Swordsmen of Client Service: Respect, Empathy, Action, and Communication."

"Yes, Grasshopper," the Master said, smiling. "But tell me what you have learned about these Four Swordsmen."

"The first two Swordsmen, Respect and Empathy, come with you when you first see a Client—while the Client is still only a Prospective Client," the younger man began. "Showing the Client Respect, you win his Respect, and then your talk of services you might provide may continue. Respect must stay with the Client, even after you're gone," explained the Young Professional.

"Yes," said the Master, "and what of Empathy?"

"Empathy must stand with you at all times," continued the Young Professional. "His sword has two edges—the one we discussed last time, which shows a Client that you like him—and the other, which listens actively and stands in the Client's shoes with him."

"Good," said the Master. "Too many salespeople practice 'Waiting-to-Talk' Listening," he added. "They are too busy thinking of their response to be standing in the Client's shoes."

"Action," declared the Young Professional, confidently now, "means to do what you say you will do."

"This is true," added the Master. "This Swordsman also carries a weapon with two sides: One understands how to Underpromise and Overdeliver, and the other understands that the Smallest Action is worth many times more than the Greatest Intention."

The Young Professional nodded in agreement. He knew these concepts well.

"What then, of Communication?" the Master asked.

"Communication is, I believe, Master, the most powerful of the Four Swordsmen for building Trust with a Client," the Young Professional said thoughtfully. "Communication of information—whether good or bad—is what the Client most wants. This Swordsman has failed when the Client must call for information the Professional has promised, rather than hearing from the Professional first—or, better still, *before* the date by which it was promised."

"And if Communication has failed?" asked the Master.

"Oh, Master," groaned the Young Professional playfully, "if any one of the Four Swordsmen of Customer Service fails, there can be no Trust. Without Trust, all of the Liking in the world will not help the Professional keep the Client."

The Master appeared to the Young Professional to be staring deeply into the younger man's soul. The Young Professional bowed silently in respect, and the Master, "seeing" this, returned his bow.

Suppose "WWD" (What We Do) and "WIIFM" (What's In It For Me) were two radio stations. Which one do you think your prospect would rather listen to?

David Frey

Tune to *Their* Station... WII-FM

Whether you're making a sale, asking for a referral, or interviewing for a position, the people you work with are usually tuned to one station — WIIFM ("What's in it for me?").

"I'm not getting enough of the people I sit down with to hire me," Rick, a financial advisor, told me.

"I keep getting job interviews," Mara, a Call Center trainer who is a casualty of a recent economic downturn, exclaimed, "but I don't get offers."

In both cases, I discovered the same problem:

They spent their time talking about their skills, their abilities, and their experience, with too little of the time devoted to discussing what the prospective client and employer needed.

Rick was proud of — and spoke eloquently about — his licensing and certification, his list of prominent clients, and his assets under management. Mara spoke about her accomplishment-packed resume.

"Be Impressed, Not Impressive," was one of Dale Carnegie's rules for successfully connecting with people in his classic book, *How to Win Friends and Influence People.*

I suggested to Rick that he would do much better if he started his interview—and spent most of it—engaged in conversation about his prospect:

> "I'd like to spend most of our time during this meeting finding out about you, if that's okay. I'm guessing you had something specific on your mind when we set up this appointment. Why don't we start with that?"

I suggested to Mara that she learn as much as she could about each company and their training departments before her appointments. Then, I advised her to spend more time on the interview asking her interviewers about what they're doing as a company and what they were looking for in a trainer than talking about herself.

A few days later, I heard from both Rick and Mara. Rick landed a new client—a local doctor he had been hoping to work with. Mara received her first job offer.

Be Impressed, Not Impressive. Spend most of your time with someone making him or her feel that you're tuned into his or her station, and you're bound to have better results.

FIFTEEN

Make It About Value, NOT Price

WHEN I'M TRAINING ENTREPRENEURS I TELL THEM THAT GOOD SELLING MEANS ASKING QUESTIONS AND LISTENING TO THE CUSTOMER. I TELL THEM, "IF YOU TALK FOR MORE THAN ONE-THIRD OF THE DISCUSSION, THEN YOU ARE SELLING BADLY."

Neil Rackham

Blake, an attorney in Michigan, explained his problem getting prospective clients to engage his services:

"I find out what their situation is," he writes, "and then I explain very carefully what I'll be doing for them."

"Then they ask about price. I tell them my hourly rate, which is competitive, but they say they want to think about it... and then, I don't hear from them again."

Professionals like Blake often don't spend enough time developing a relationship with their clients, customers, or patients. They know their work. They know how to diagnose problems, and they know what the most likely solutions are. But they don't know what their prospective clients really clients really need: Someone to hear them out; sympathy, empathy, and validation.

Here are some suggestions that might help you "close" more clients:

1. **Go deeper with your questions.** "Situation" questions are essential for you in order to enable you to do your work, but they have relatively low value to a prospective client who already knows her situation.

   How does her situation make her feel? Why does she feel that way? What result would she like to see from working with you? How will that make her feel better?

The answers to these kinds of questions don't necessarily add anything for you to analyze, but they help you to create a bond with your prospective client.

2. **Find out if there's a perception of your value before you talk about fees.** Ask if she's receiving value from the discussion, and if she has questions for you. Ask if she'd be interested in having you work with her.

3. **Find out what is causing her to hesitate.** If she says, "Let me think about it," find out what she agrees with, and narrow down what her concerns are. Does she have reservations about your abilities? Is she looking for a better price? It's okay (it's important) to ask these questions.

If you want more clients to say "yes," try changing your interview style by asking more and deeper questions. When you uncover a problem or need, ask your prospect about his or her feelings about that need. As the interview is coming to a close, find out if he or she feels that value has been provided (through your questions and focused listening).

When you ask if your prospect would like to engage you, if there is hesitation, ask more questions about it. This will allow you to develop that essential relationship with your client, customer, or patient.

81

THE ROYAL ROAD TO A MAN'S HEART IS TO TALK TO HIM ABOUT THE THINGS HE TREASURES MOST.

Dale Carnegie

Memorize this Simple Triplet

One of the Internet Marketing "gurus" I follow, Frank Kern, recently summed up *Internet Marketing* in three sentences:

Here's what I got...

Here's what it will do for you...

Here's what I want you to do next...

It struck me that this simple—if grammatically incorrect—triplet is at the core of everything about which I coach professionals and their sales teams, when we are working on attracting clients. Let me explain:

Here's what I got. Once you have a prospect who needs your services, you can describe the **Features** of your offering.

This car is equipped with an Acme "Sound-Around" fifteen-hundred-jigawatt stereo.

Here's what it will do for you. This is where you talk about two types of results you can get from the Features: **Advantages** and **Benefits**. Advantages are the results anyone might get. Professionals who are amateurs at selling their services will stop with these.

An Advantage looks something like this:

If you buy this car with this sound system, you can expect the clearest, most beautiful sound you've ever heard.

Benefits are the *ultimate results* that this particular client is looking for. One person might want that clear sound because he wants to follow the guitar riff of his favorite guitarist while he drives. Another might want it because he is irritated by noise pollution outside and needs something soothing in his car. These are Benefits. The best professional sales are made not from talking about Advantages, but from talking about Benefits:

Having that beautiful, clear music will give you what you told me you were looking for in your new car. It will soothe you, so that you're at your absolute best when you arrive at each appointment.

The only way to know what clients consider a Benefit is through thoughtful, caring questions about what they need, and about why that need is important to them.

Here's what I want you to do next. This is the **Call to Action** — what the guys in the loud plaid jackets call "the close." Contrary to what they might tell you, the way you word your

Call to Action is just not that important if you've helped your prospective client understand, through your questions, that he or she really needs the Benefits of what you're offering. You just have to ask them what they need to do next:

Would you like to get started with the paperwork?

Use this triplet when you're thinking about your practice or business, and the features of your services, and ask your prospective clients lots of questions. Then, show them not just the Advantages, but also the Benefits of your service.

IN ORDER TO SUCCEED, YOUR DESIRE FOR SUCCESS SHOULD BE GREATER THAN YOUR FEAR OF FAILURE.

Bill Cosby

Help Them WIN Gold Medals and Avoid Alligators

SEVENTEEN

In the Great Swamp Race, two runners led the pack.

Fred was running this grueling race through the alligator-infested swamp—past twisted vines, muck, and mire—motivated by his desire to cross the finish line first, and win the gold medal. Ed, on the other hand, had started out with the same intention, but his speed and determination at the moment were motivated mainly by his desire not to be eaten by the alligators.

If you were selling running shoes to Fred, your best approach would be to help him picture the glory of crossing the finish line ahead of the pack. But Ed would not respond to that effort at all. To sell running shoes to Ed, you would have to talk about the alligators.

If you are selling services to a potential client or patient, or if you're selling an idea to your employer, you probably have been selling only gold medals—talking about all the wonderful things to be gained by accepting your offer:

This will help you retire comfortably.

This will get you the best possible price.

This will make you feel great.

But if you sell only gold medals, you will miss out on all of the people who are running from alligators. For them, your message should be more like:

This will keep you from having to go back to work a few years after you retire.

This will help keep you from feeling trapped into accepting terrible offers.

This will keep you from feeling run down.

The problem is that you often don't know whether your prospective client is concerned with gold medals or alligators. While you can try to find out by asking great questions, why not simply try addressing <u>both</u>?

This will help you retire comfortably, and you will never have to worry about going back to work after you do.

This will get you the best possible price, so you will never have to feel trapped into accepting terrible offers.

This will make you feel great; you will never have to feel run down again.

Want to get ahead in your business, or not be left behind at work? Talk about both gold medals and alligators.

Part 4: Dos and Don'ts

PEOPLE HATE TO BE SOLD, BUT THEY LOVE TO BUY.

Jeffrey Gitomer

EIGHTEEN

Are you aggressively selling your services and finding that few prospective clients—even those who are clearly in your target market—are buying?

Or, maybe you're struggling to find new clients because you're afraid that if you reach out to people you'll appear to be *selling*—something you just can't bring yourself to do?

The Solution is to STOP SELLING!

Earlier in this book, I talked about the negative view many professionals have of selling:

~ Trying to convince someone to buy what you offer

~ Manipulating someone into thinking he or she has a need for what you offer

If your view of selling your services is something along these lines, it's no wonder that you can't fill your practice or find enough clients for your business. If this is your view,

STOP *SELLING* YOUR SERVICES!

Develop an "attraction" mindset. What you offer is something valuable, something people want or need. If you have any clients at all, you've already proved that. People need to know about your practice or business. You should be proud to tell them about it. But you don't have to "push" it on them.

Resist the urge to sell, and ask great questions instead. The *selling* that doesn't work usually involves some type of "show up and throw up" approach. You find a prospect and proceed to tell them all about you and how great you are. You don't feel right, and neither do they.

Instead, tell a prospective client what you do, and then ask his permission to explore his situation. The conversation might end right there, but since people do like to buy, but not to be sold—and you're *not selling*—he's likely to agree to let you explore. Once you have permission, ask questions designed to unearth some specific need or desire.

Address the specific need or desire. Explore that need or desire deeply. Then, instead of talking about generic features and advantages of your service, discuss how what you do meets that specific need or desire, addressing the values you've uncovered.

Rick owns a cleaning service franchise. He wanted to get more of the people he met during his various "networking" activities to agree to let him give them an estimate. More often than not, he somehow put them off.

Rick demonstrated how he'd start a conversation, find out where the person he was speaking to lived, and then make his move:

"Mary, I'd love to come out to your home next week and give you an estimate. What day is best for you?"

After some coaching, Rick's conversations went more like this:

Rick: *It's basically a residential service, Mary. Do you mind if I ask... do you have a cleaning service?*

Mary: *No. It's not that I wouldn't like to have one; it's just that they're so expensive, and we're really not in a position to afford one.*

Rick: *Do the two of you have children?*

Mary: *Yes, three. They're all school age, and they do help with the cleaning, but they have so much homework to do.*

Rick: *And you work, too, right? Well, if the cost weren't a big issue, how would a cleaning service help?*

Mary: *Are you kidding? It would cut 4 – 5 hours out of my week.*

Rick: *That sounds great. What would you do with that extra time?*

Mary: *Well my little one, Tina, needs help with her homework, and I'm always trying to squeeze out an extra few minutes for her here or there.*

Rick: *It sounds like you don't have the time you need to help Tina. I can't promise that I can make it affordable for you, but would it make sense to get an estimate for cleaning, and discuss the different ways we might free up some time for you to work with Tina? How about sometime next week?*

Using this "attraction approach,", rather than selling, Rick was able to triple his appointments in just a few weeks. He was amazed by how easy it was to get people to say "yes."

NINETEEN

Help Your Clients Be HEROES

YOUR CLIENTS KNOW COLLEAGUES, FRIENDS, AND THEIR CUSTOMERS WHO WILL BENEFIT FROM KNOWING YOU… ASKING FOR REFERRALS, IN ALL ITS FORMS, SERVES YOUR CLIENTS BY HELPING THEM HELP OTHERS.

Bill Cates

Lawyers tremble at the thought of it. Financial advisors and entrepreneurs avoid it whenever they can. Coaches blush when I bring up the subject. Medical professionals proclaim it's beneath them, so they won't have to do it. Even when I show them how to do it, they find ways to avoid it. What is this unthinkable task? Asking for referrals.

Why don't they ask? Either they're really afraid (*What if my client gets the impression that I'm needy and thinks less of me for asking? What if she grabs back her retainer check and storms out of the room?*), or they just don't know that it's okay to ask, and don't know how to do it comfortably.

What these professionals fail to understand is that there are reasons why their clients would *want* to refer them to someone else.

Years ago, Police Captain Myron taught me about the "hero factor" in the referral process. Myron, who tipped the scale beyond the 300-pound line, and was known to consume more than his fair share of alcohol, was at a party to which both he and I had been invited. At one point during the party, he threw one huge arm around my shoulders and announced to the entire room, "You see this guy? I brought him all his business."

It was true that Captain Myron had introduced me to several clients. I thought it wise not to argue that most of my business came from other sources. But what I came to understand that evening was how important it was to Captain Myron to be the champion of my practice—to be a hero.

Here's how it works:

1. People generally like to help one another. If a client likes you and believes you add value to his businesses or to his life, helping you will make him feel generous and important.

2. More importantly, when your client is referring you to someone with whom she has a connection, it's an opportunity for her to show the people whose opinions are important to her that she makes wise decisions—decisions that can help them, too. In other words, she can be a hero to them.

People want their presence on earth to have meaning. They want to make a difference in someone's life or someone's business. They want to be heroes to someone. When you're not asking clients to introduce you to business associates, friends, and family members you might be able to help (in the same way you're helping them), you're actually depriving them of the opportunity to be a hero.

Asking clients to refer you to the people in their lives also gives them something else they need—validation. What they're thinking is, "If my sister uses your services, too, she must see in you what I saw. Then I know I made a good decision going to you after all."

Don't deprive your clients of the opportunity to be heroes. Ask them to introduce you to people you can help in the same way you're helping them.

OBJECTIONS AREN'T ROADBLOCKS, RED FLAGS, OR STOP SIGNS. THEY'RE AN OPPORTUNITY TO LEARN MORE ABOUT YOUR PROSPECT'S TRUTH SO YOU AND THEY CAN DECIDE WHETHER THE SOLUTION YOU'RE OFFERING CAN SOLVE THEIR PROBLEM OR ISSUE.

Ari Galper

TWENTY

STOP "Handling" Objections

You're trying to get a prospective client to meet with you, to purchase services from you, or to recommend you to an associate, and you suddenly find yourself facing resistance. The old sales model many professionals use calls this an "objection" and suggests that you "handle" it, which basically means to argue it down.

"Your fees seem high," a prospective client says. So, you jump to defend those fees. That's handling them:

"Well, we're the best at what we do, and you can find it for less, but you get what you pay for," might be the response under the old model. This defensive, argumentative response is not likely to bring about a change for the better in the prospective client's opinion, and might even have the opposite effect. You're trying to swat down the "objection", and that approach doesn't work very often.

A more effective approach would be to *bend* with any resistance you sense in your conversation:

> "Well, you know, Joe, you're right. I suppose it can appear that way if you haven't experienced the level and quality of service we bring our clients. How important is it to you to get the best quality and the best service?"

The key to getting more clients to say "yes" is to *remove resistance or stress* whenever you sense it's there, and bending with it is often a much more effective approach.

TWENTY-ONE

Dump the Sales TALK

SHORTEN YOUR COLD CALLING OPENER TO JUST THE ESSENTIAL RESULTS THAT YOU PROVIDE, AND THEN GET RIGHT INTO PROBING FOR PROBLEMS. YOU'LL SELL MORE THIS WAY.

Shamus Brown

Call me crazy, but when someone calls me on the phone to try to sell me something, I don't hang up on him or her. I listen and respond, and then make suggestions to the caller about how to improve his or her call.

For many people, prospecting—marketing—for new clients on the telephone, or "cold calling," is the job of last resort. Who wants to be cursed at, hung up on, and lied to? But many of my clients are in professions where cold calling is one of their necessary methods of prospecting for new business.

Do people hate to receive calls at home? Do busy managers and executives hate to be bothered by callers trying to convince them to buy their products? Yes… and… No.

"If I were calling you to tell you that you just *actually* inherited a million dollars, and I needed to arrange for you to pick up the check," I ask in my workshops, "would you be angry that I interrupted your dinner?"

"No," they all agree.

"If I were calling you at your place of business with a *guaranteed* way to make more money while simultaneously reducing expenses," I ask, "would you be upset that I got past your 'gatekeeper' to reach you?"

"No," they eventually agree again, with just a touch of skepticism.

"So, then," I ask, "what do your prospects hate?"

The answer usually comes down to calls from "telemarketers" or from salespeople who sound like telemarketers. There are, of course, successful telemarketers who sound natural and comfortable, but you know the type I'm talking about….

~ They mispronounce your name with no apology and no effort to get it right.

~ They sound like they're reading a script.

~ They come on strong, forcing a big "salesy" smile through the telephone.

~ They try to warm up the call by pausing to say or ask something disingenuous like, "And How Are You Today, Mr. [badly mispronounced name]?" You know they don't care at all about your health or well being.

~ They use "salesy" language like, "We're going to be in your neighborhood on Tuesday" or "This is an exclusive offer."

If part of your work is making calls to people you don't know, the "telemarketer type" provides you a great guideline for how not to do it.

Here are some suggestions for how to do it right:

1. Get the name right beforehand or apologize and fix it. If you can't find out how to pronounce the prospect's name ahead of time, ask if you got it right. Apologize and try again. Continuing to call me "Mr. Skuzzel" won't help your cause.

2. Throw away the script—one way or another. Scripts are okay. Some of the best actors use them. But you change the channel quickly when the actor sounds like he or she is reading it. Either learn it so well that you no longer sound like you're reading it, or toss it away.

Instead, keep an outline with the bullet points of the things you want to say. It's not a bad idea to keep it near you, but don't read it.

3. Forget about the old rule that says you should sound "up" when you call. Coming on too strong can be a turnoff. Don't be timid, but start gently—and adjust to the person you're talking with.

4. Don't do AHAYT. "And How Are You Today?" raises an instant red flag for me that I'm going to be sorry I took this call, so just don't do it. Get to the point of your call. Telemarketers use this greeting to catch their breath before jumping into the script—and prospects know it. Another killer these days is "actually" as in "Actually, the reason I'm calling is . . ."

5. Stay away from "salesy" language. "We're going to be in your neighborhood" is a sales-killer. If you're seeing someone "up the street" or you name the town, you have a better chance of getting an appointment than if you will happen to be "in my neighborhood."

Perhaps the most important change you can make is in your focus. Make cold calling more fun for you and less painful for your prospective clients by aiming not for the appointment or sale, but to engage them in conversation—to develop relationships. While this may, at first glance, seem like the long way to go about it, I promise that it will be much more effective.

WE TELL LIES WHEN
WE ARE AFRAID...
AFRAID OF WHAT
WE DON'T KNOW,
AFRAID OF WHAT
OTHERS WILL THINK,
AFRAID OF WHAT WILL
BE FOUND OUT ABOUT US.

BUT EVERY TIME WE TELL A LIE,
THE THING THAT WE FEAR
GROWS STRONGER.

Tad Williams

TWENTY-TWO

Stop Telling Lies

"When an old inactive client on my list won't respond to my calls and letters," a financial professional at a recent workshop told the group, "I send a card confirming our appointment—an appointment we don't have—and that gets them to call me."

"But that's a lie," I responded. "You're using a lie to get them to call you."

"So?" the indignant advisor shot back. "Clients lie all the time."

While she was right that clients are, of course, often less than truthful about the things they tell us; the idea that it was, therefore, okay for a professional to lie in order to get an appointment or to close a sale—bothered me.

A few days later, I came across an e-mail from a colleague, Ari Galper, complaining that somewhere along the line it seems to have become okay for sellers to lie. Only we don't call them lies, Ari complained; we call them techniques:

"I'm conducting a survey..." (when you're really not).

"I was going to be in your neighborhood..." (when you really weren't going to be).

"I'm confirming our appointment..." (when there is none).

"There are just two left..." (when there are plenty left).

Many of the so-called "client development gurus" are teaching professionals that the end (getting the client) justifies the means (saying anything, without regard for the truth). It's no wonder that the professionals and entrepreneurs who find their way to me tell me that when they hear the word "sales" they run for cover.

In growing your business or practice, the end never justifies the means. Tell your clients and prospects the truth so that they'll have a reason to trust you. They may be in the habit of lying to you, but it will be easier to get to their truths if you are being authentic.

The advisor who addressed the group at my workshop was proud of the fact that her lie compelled these inactive clients to communicate with her—something they had previously refused to do. The lie got them to contact her, but I could almost promise that they went back to being inactive immediately after they did. Or, they became ex-clients entirely. If I were the client, I'd be firmly convinced that the lie she told to get my attention justified my decision not to keep working with her.

You'll get more clients when you take the pressure off of yourself to play games with the truth.

TWENTY-THREE

DON'T Be a Stalker

TOO MUCH OF A GOOD THING IS NOT A GOOD THING

Jay Leno

"I just read about Alicia, and how reluctant she was to promote her business," Jeanie, a long-time subscriber wrote me, in response to an article on persistence in my Blog. (Alicia's story is in the next chapter.) "But what about someone who is *too* persistent?"

> "We know a husband and wife real estate team who are aware we have no interest in selling our house. They call to ask for referrals; they drop off gifts. (The latest was a birdseed bell, which was actually something we put in our yard; but we still found it annoying that they came to drop it off at our house.) They send personalized letters almost every week, and they send homeowner tips monthly. And they call—all the time. When we catch their names on the caller ID we let it go to voice mail. Every week or two is just too much!"

Persistence is a good thing... until it becomes annoying. Jeanie and her husband will go out of their way not to call these realtors if, and when, the time comes to sell their home—so all this incredible effort will have been counter-productive.

Jeanie's realtors are trying to develop a relationship using mass marketing techniques and are bound to fail. Business and referral relationships are built on respect and trust, not contact volume. Let's look at what these realtors are doing:

1. **Asking about interest**. There was nothing wrong with asking—the first time. Follow-ups, however, should have been *permission*-based:

   "Jeanie, Joe, would it be okay if we followed up with you in three months to see if anything has changed?"

2. **Asking for referrals.** I teach and encourage every professional to ask for referrals, but one of the immutable referral rules is to ask only after you have determined whether your clients perceive that they have received value from you. It would be okay to ask Jeanie and Joe if they know someone who might be thinking of selling, but to keep asking when there has been no value given or perceived is self-sabotage.

3. **Dropping off gifts**. Bringing a gift when you first call on someone is a good idea. Even if they see the gift as an attempt to "buy" their favor, who can resist a gift? But dropping  off gifts on a regular basis can make you look desperate. Jeanie and Joe are using the birdseed ball, but they won't be using the realtors, so only the birds benefit from this effort.

4. **Letters and monthly tips.** The weekly letters from the realtors are another example of using mass-marketing techniques in a futile attempt to create a relationship. Monthly newsletters or "tip sheets" are a wonderful idea, but here again, only if they are permission-based. All these realtors needed to do was to ask:

   "Jeanie and Joe, we have a great letter we send to people monthly with tips for increasing the value of their homes, but we wouldn't want to send it unless you think you might have an interest in it. Would you like to be on our list?"

5. **Constant calling.** This one doesn't need an expert opinion. It's one of the reasons people put themselves on "Do Not Call" lists. Jeanie and Joe are trying to be polite because the realtors are a local couple, but the realtors have made them prisoners to their Caller ID.

If these realtors want Jeanie and Joe to work with them and refer people to them, they need to develop a relationship with them based on respect for their privacy, and with permission. They need to find ways to give Jeanie and Joe real value instead of showering them with calls and gifts that reinforce the idea that they're more interested in themselves than they are in Jeanie and Joe.

Part 5: It's Easy... Just Do It!

YOU KNOW THE VALUE OF EVERY MERCHANDISE, BUT YOU DO NOT KNOW YOUR OWN VALUE— THAT IS STUPIDITY.

The Sufi Path of Love,
The Spiritual Teaching of Rumi

TWENTY-FOUR

Be Clear on YOUR Value

"You want me to call up my previous clients, just to see how they're doing?" my client Alicia asked me two weeks ago. She was astonished that I would suggest something so forward.

"Isn't that unprofessional—or unethical?" she asked.

"Do you care how they're doing now?" I asked her.

"Well, of course I do," came the reply.

"Why, then, would it be wrong to check up on them periodically?" I asked.

Alicia has been a coach for four years, helping young professionals with career transitions. She had consulted me because she wanted to grow her business. Her belief system was that she needed to maintain her professional distance; and her interpretation of what that meant included the idea that once clients had benefited from her services and ended the coaching relationship, she no longer had a reason to communicate with those clients.

Alicia agreed to call four of her clients, just to see how they were doing, and report back to me. She even agreed to ask them to tell her the value she brought to their careers and to their lives.

A week later, Alicia called me back. As soon as we connected on the phone, she couldn't wait for our "hellos" to end to tell me about her experiences.

"First of all, they were grateful that I cared enough to follow-up," she began. "None of them thought, as I did last week, that my call was inappropriate."

"That got me comfortable enough to ask them about the value they received from me," she continued proudly, "and that's what I'm really excited about."

Alicia found out that she had given each of her clients confidence, focus, and someone to hold them accountable until they were on their feet again.

It reinforced all of her beliefs in what she was doing and got her excited about finding more clients. So excited, that she was able to do the one thing she had been unable to bring herself to agree to do the week before.

"I said to each of them, 'Don't keep me a secret,' as you had suggested," Alicia announced proudly. "And right there on the phone, one of them told me about a friend she was going to talk to who she thought could use my help."

Here's what Alicia learned:

~ If you have former clients whose experiences with you were positive, stay in touch with them. An e-mail or phone call at the right time could mean a lot to them.

~ Ask them about why they chose you and your firm, and what value they received from working with you.

~ Don't be afraid to mention that you're open to introductions to other people who may need your help. Simple statements like "Don't keep me a secret" or "I'm never too busy to help someone you care about" can open the door to new clients.

CREATE A DEFINITE PLAN FOR
CARRYING OUT YOUR DESIRE
AND BEGIN AT ONCE,
WHETHER YOU ARE READY
OR NOT, TO PUT THIS PLAN
INTO ACTION

Napoleon Hill

TWENTY-FIVE

Ask, Believe, and Take Action

A few Christmases ago, I sent some of my clients a video produced in Australia called *The Secret*, based on a book by Rhonda Byrne. At the time, the book and video were still pretty much a secret.

A few months later, Oprah discovered *The Secret*, after which the stores couldn't keep the book or the video in stock. But as is true with so many of the success principles that are being repackaged daily into books, the ideas in *The Secret*—though powerful—are not new.

The secret of *The Secret* is that there is a law as fundamental as the law of gravity—the Law of Attraction. The basis for this "Law" is that thoughts are things. When you're thinking about something you want, the thoughts are going out into the Universe and creating that thing for you.

If you (1) ASK the universe for something—expressing your desire loudly and clearly—and you continue to focus on it, and you (2) BELIEVE that it will come to you, you will (3) RECEIVE it.

This is not a new idea; nor is it a secret only a few privileged people know. It's just great packaging of a powerful self-help concept that I have been coaching clients to accept for years, particularly where growing their businesses or improving their careers is concerned. In 1937, in *Think and Grow Rich,* Napoleon Hill wrote:

What the mind of man can conceive and believe, it can achieve.

But as Napoleon Hill makes clear in his book, and as I've seen it work, there's another element that is currently being glossed over—the need to *take action.* Every one of the famous, rich, powerful people mentioned in these books took action on his or her desire. They found that it is not enough to ask and believe, no matter how focused and intense you are. You need to have a plan of action and to act on that plan.

I have seen the Law of Attraction work hundreds of times for me, and for my clients—but not simply because they wished more business into the office, or believed that the telephone would ring. Wishing and believing *accompanied by action,* however, works!

The proof that there is something to *The Secret* is that many of the clients who have had success in attracting what they wanted into their businesses—and into their lives—received it from a different source than the one they were pursuing.

In my book, *The High Diving Board,* I tell the story of my flight from Princeton, New Jersey to Santa Rosa, California to try to convince an author I admired to let me work for him as a speaker or trainer. It did not work out. But while I was out in California, I received a call from NYU's Marketing and Management Institute inviting me to come teach a course to entrepreneurs. I received something I wanted from a different source than the one I was pursuing. This could have only happened because I (1) ASKED the universe for what I wanted, (2) BELIEVED it would happen somehow, and (3) TOOK ACTION, of some kind, to get it.

HOW CAN YOU HAVE CHARISMA? BE MORE CONCERNED ABOUT MAKING OTHERS FEEL GOOD ABOUT THEMSELVES THAN YOU ARE MAKING THEM FEEL GOOD ABOUT YOU.

Dan Reiland

TWENTY-SIX

Exercise YOUR Charisma Muscle

"Charisma" helps you attract clients. But is it something that—as a client suggested a while ago—you simply have or don't, or is it something you can develop?

Watching TV as Barack Obama connected with the crowd of 80,000 Democrats in the stadium on a Thursday night before the 2008 election, the word "charisma" came to mind. I'm not making a political statement here—most of the candidates have it: that ability to "light up" a room when they walk into it.

Webster defines charisma as "a personal magnetism." It was  originally a religious term, meaning "of the spirit" or "inspired"—the idea that God's light was shining through someone. So, charismatic people have the ability to let their light shine.

But if it is something you can *develop*, how can you start? Here are seven ways the experts say you can boost your "Charisma Factor":

1. **Have a mission.** What do you stand for? What is your purpose? What is the message you consistently send out to the world? If you have one, and you're living by it every day, people will see your charismatic light.

2. **Be passionate about your work.** Professionals with charisma are leaders in their field. Others will turn to them when an important issue is is being discussed, and their passion for their subject will shine through.

3. **Project confidence.** While some charismatic people are "big" and loud, most have a calm, assertive manner. You can sense their confidence when you first meet them, and it attracts you. While there are some exceptions, most clients will find these qualities in a professional charismatic.

4. **Be bold, but humble.** Charismatic people know how to balance talking about their accomplishments with being grateful for—and humbled by—the praise they receive.

5. **Develop a personal style.** Mark Twain quipped that "naked people have little or no influence on society." If your professional uniform is a buttoned-down blue pin-striped suit, but that's not who you are, go ahead and wear that big Mickey Mouse watch proudly.

6. **Be happy.** Happy people generally generate more magnetism than those who appear unhappy. Happy professionals tend to have more clients and more satisfied clients. If you're unhappy, get some help to change your situation. It will improve your charisma.

7. **Derive joy from others.** A sincere interest in, and concern for, other people is a charismatic quality. Watch someone you think is charismatic, and you'll see it.

Charisma comes more easily to some than to others, but anyone who develops these skills can become more charismatic.

THE PROBLEM IS THAT MOST
PEOPLE FOCUS ON THEIR
FAILURES RATHER THAN
THEIR SUCCESSES.
BUT THE TRUTH IS THAT
MOST PEOPLE HAVE
MANY MORE SUCCESSES
THAN FAILURES.

Jack Canfield

TWENTY-SEVEN

Focus on Where YOU Want to Go, Not the Wall!

If you're racing toward a curve, and you focus on the wall you don't want to hit—you'll probably hit it.

Race car drivers like Scott Dixon and Jimmie Johnson know that whether it's a wall or a car wreck in front of you, your focus needs to be on the open road ahead of them, not the obstacle.

This idea has been on my mind lately as the news focuses on frightened investors selling their shares of stock at plummeting prices. One thing people tend to forget about the stock market is that you can't sell your shares unless there's a buyer for them. Someone is purchasing all those discounted stock shares being sold every day by people focused on the abyss.

Those purchasers are taking the view that the economy will improve at some point; and if they buy great stocks at deep discounts now, when it does improve, they'll be way ahead of where they were last year and the year before. They're looking at future economic growth, not at the wrecked economy.

My purpose here, however, is not to give you investment advice. It's to show you that while external events beyond our control—like the current economic crisis or accidents on the racetrack—do throw roadblocks in our way, the people who continue to have success are the ones who focus on their goals, not on the mess they're hoping to avoid.

I hear struggling professionals focused on their walls every day:

"The economy is killing my business."

"Recruiting for new salespeople is impossible."

"No one is buying [my kind of service] right now."

When you focus on where you want to go instead of the wall, what you say sounds more like this:

"I'm working on ways that I can help clients through this tough period and still grow my business."

"I'm speaking to more people than usual to compensate for the tough recruiting environment."

"I'm finding ways to entice people to buy [my kind of service].

Don't hit the wall or become part of whatever wreckage is on the road in front of you. Focus on where you want to go, and you'll have a lot better chance of getting there.

About the Author

More than 30 years ago, Sandy Schussel started a law practice that grew quickly, through the application of what he now calls "client attraction systems." After several years of practice, he discovered that his passion was for getting and keeping clients, and teaching others to do the same, but not for doing legal work.

After a year-long battle with cancer in 1992, Sandy was faced with the prospect of rebuilding the practice for which he had no passion, or instead, pursuing the work he loved.

Since that time, Sandy has been working with individuals and organizations throughout the United States to teach them to attract all of the quality clients they want, regardless of economic conditions. He has worked extensively with financial advisors, attorneys, and service businesses and their teams, and has helped them to produce dramatic results.

Sandy's first book, *The High Diving Board: How To Overcome Your Fears and Live Your Dreams*, acknowledges that one of the greatest barriers to success for professionals of all types, including sales professionals, is fear. He provides a ten-step system for overcoming this significant barrier that has helped thousands of people take their first steps to a better career and a better life.

You can find out more about Sandy's work, along with some helpful business tools, at his website, **www.brassringcoaching.com,** where you can also sign up for his popular Newsletter and Blog, *REACHING...* Or visit the Blog directly at **www.brassringcoachingblog.com**.

Robert D. Reed Publishers Order Form

Call in your order for fast service and quantity discounts
(541) 347- 9882

OR order on-line at **www.rdrpublishers.com** *using PayPal.*
OR order by mail:
Make a copy of this form; enclose payment information:
Robert D. Reed Publishers
1380 Face Rock Drive, Bandon, OR 97411
Note: Shipping is $3.50 1st book + $1 for each additional book.
Send indicated books to:

Name _____

Address _____

City _____ State _____ Zip _____

Phone _____ Fax _____ Cell _____

E-Mail_____
Payment by check ☐ or credit card ☐ *(All major credit cards are accepted.)*

Name on card _____

Card Number _____

Exp. Date _____ Last 3-Digit number on back of card _____

Become a Client Magnet: <u>*Qty.*</u>
27 Strategies to Boost Your Client-Attraction Factor
by Sandy Schussel...$11.95 _____

The Joy of Selling
by Steve Chandler...$11.95 _____

100 Ways to Create Wealth
by Steve Chandler & Sam Beckford ....$24.95 _____

Ten Commitments to Your Success
by Steve Chandler...$11.95 _____

Customer Astonishment:
10 Secrets to World-Class Customer Care
by Darby Checketts...$14.95 _____

The New American Prosperity: Redefining Success
as Smart and Happy versus Rich and Famous
by Darby Checketts...$12.95 _____

Other book title(s) from www.rdrpublishers.com:

_____ $_____

_____ $_____